For my father

Bill Hess

You first took me to New York and
opened my eyes to all that was possible

New York

—

THROUGH A FASHION EYE

Megan Hess

hardie grant books

Contents

Listings

Acknowledgements

—

To Meelee Soorkia, thank you for being the best editor a fashion illustrator could ever dream of! Our third book together and it still feels like we are having far too much fun to ever call this work. It still amazes me that you are both highly creative and completely rational, all at once!

To Laura Gardner, thank you for all the research you did into this book and for being a pleasure to work with. Thanks also for your persistence in seeking out all that is fashionable and fabulous.

To Martina Granolic, thank you for casting your well-tuned eye over every illustration in this book and for caring so much about every tiny detail that went into every single page.

To Murray Batten, it's always so exciting to see the amazing design you create for each of my books. It never ceases to amaze me that you can take 100 illustrations and piles of text and make them come to life in the most beautiful visual story.

To Justine Clay, thank you for encouraging and supporting my work from the very beginning. Without you taking me under your wing in New York, this book wouldn't exist. I will always consider meeting you being like winning the lottery!

To my husband Craig, thank you for supporting every little dream of mine and for sharing my love of adventure in The Big Apple.

To my two children, Gwyn and Will. At the end of the day you both make everything more fun and in your own little ways you inspire me to always do the best I can.

About the author

—

Megan Hess was destined to draw. An initial career in graphic design evolved into art direction for some of the world's leading design agencies. In 2008, Hess illustrated the *New York Times* number one selling book, *Sex and the City*, written by Candace Bushnell. She has since illustrated portraits for *Vanity Fair* and *Time*, created iconic illustrations for Cartier in Paris, animations for Prada in Milan and illustrated the windows of Bergdorf Goodman in New York.

Hess's signature style can also be found on her bespoke limited edition prints and homewares sold around the globe. Her renowned clients include Chanel, Dior, Tiffany & Co., Yves Saint Laurent, Vogue, Harpers Bazaar, Cartier, Balmain, Montblanc, Wedgewood and Prada.

When she's not in her studio working, you'll find her perched in a cosy Manhattan café secretly drawing all the chic New Yorkers around her.

Visit Megan at **meganhess.com**

Introduction

—

I've been in love with the city that never sleeps since my first visit as a teenager. I remember the morning I arrived in New York on a chilly winter's day in March. The air was freezing, and steam bellowed up from the streets. The sky was filled with more skyscrapers than I had ever seen, honking cabs flew past and chic New Yorkers strutted the sidewalks. This was the Manhattan I had always imagined and I was so excited to finally be there.

Each year after that I would travel back to New York with a tiny suitcase and big dreams of establishing a creative career in that amazing city. In 2006, on one of those trips, I met Justine Clay, the woman who would become a mentor and my agent. Justine was the first person to truly believe in my work; she took me under her wing and shared my portfolio of illustrations with the creative elite of Manhattan.

My big break came with a heart-stopping commission from Candace Bushnell's publisher; Candace wanted me to illustrate the cover of *Sex and the City*. It was a dream project that would lead to many more, firmly placing my work in New York and helping me to realise my childhood dream of becoming a fashion illustrator.

Since then I've illustrated for clients in New York such as Tiffany & Co, New York Fashion Week, *Time* and *Vanity Fair* magazines, Henri Bendel, Elizabeth Arden, Bloomingdale's, and Bergdorf Goodman. I've even had the honour of illustrating portraits of Michelle Obama.

Today my work takes me all around the world; I travel between hemispheres for exciting commissions that range from the size of a postage stamp to the expanse of an entire building. But I am still in contact with my Manhattan clients every day, and my heart will always be in New York.

This book is a collection of my favourite places to visit, eat, drink, stay and shop in the city, from iconic institutions to the hidden gems I've discovered on my trips over the years – such as where to get the best take-away coffee during Fashion Week, or where to shop for a pair of killer heels.

Each time I visit there's always more to see and do; New York never ceases to excite, inspire and enchant me. It was the streets of New York that I first fell in love with, but it's the fashion that keeps bringing me back.

My favourite things ...

LOUIS VUITTON BAG

TIFFANY TRAVEL WALLET

LARGE SKETCH BOOK

TRAVEL DIARY

SILK SCARF

FANCY LINGERIE

LADY DIOR

... to pack for New York

YSL SHOES FOR NIGHT

CHANEL FLATS FOR DAY

FAVOURITE SCENT

LIPSTICK DAY AND NIGHT

WATCH

LBD

STATEMENT NECKLACE

KILLER EARRINGS

CHANEL BAG

My favourite ensembles ...

SHOPPING
UPTOWN

GALLERY
OPENING

MET GALA

... for New York occasions

COCKTAILS
AND DINNER

SHOPPING
DOWNTOWN

MEETING
ANNA WINTOUR

01

Central
Park

Extending over three square kilometres between the Upper West and East Sides, Central Park is the heart of Manhattan. The park takes on a completely different life in summer and winter, and is a paradise in the middle of the city providing the perfect place to promenade and people-watch. Wander through the cherry blossoms in spring, brave the ice rink in winter or picnic in style in the summer months. Central Park is also one of the city's most popular film set locations, offering a backdrop for films such as *When Harry Met Sally, Manhattan* and *Enchanted*.

Museum of Modern Art (MoMA)

11 WEST 53RD STREET, MIDTOWN

As New York's pre-eminent gallery of modern and contemporary art, MoMA is a must for art lovers, architecture enthusiasts and tourists alike, and attracts millions of visitors each year. The stunning Midtown building was closed to the public between 2002 and 2004 while it underwent a breathtaking, air-filled expansion designed by Yoshio Taniguchi. The gallery is home to one of the most important collections of art, photography and design – including a collection of Richard Avedon's inspiring fashion photographs. But MoMA's fashion credentials really come into their own when the gallery plays host to some of the most glamorous parties in New York, like their annual garden party with a guest list that has included Anna Wintour, Cate Blanchett, Jeff Koons and Kanye West, among others.

Guggenheim

**1071 FIFTH AVENUE,
UPPER EAST SIDE**

GUGGENHEIM

Established by the influential Guggenheim family, the Solomon R. Guggenheim Museum is an essential stop for visitors to New York. The circular space-age building is itself worthy of inspection. Designed by architect Frank Lloyd Wright, it is breathtaking inside and out, and houses a collection devoted to twentieth-century modern and contemporary art, including an impressive collection of fashion photography. I love wandering down the spiralling interior of the gallery imagining the presence of Peggy Guggenheim – the famous collector known for her precocious style. Today, the building comes alive at the annual Guggenheim International Gala. The glamorous event attracts A-list fashion industry and film stars.

New York Public Library

FIFTH AVENUE AT 42ND STREET, MIDTOWN

Escape from Manhattan's concrete jungle with a visit to the city's home of books and culture: The New York Public Library. The free access library is both an architectural landmark and a social institution. Statuesque lions flank the front entrance. The library's marble foyer is awe-inspiring; it was the location of the first wedding scene in the *Sex and the City* film. In addition to all of the incredible books, art fills the library at every turn, whether it's the latest exhibition at the Gottesman Hall or the stunning ceiling of the grand Rose Main Reading Room. Even New York fashion designer and longtime library benefactor Bill Blass has a stunningly decorated Public Catalog Room dedicated to him.

Uptown
Park Avenue/
Madison Avenue/
Fifth Avenue

ridging the Upper West Side, Central Park and the Upper East Side across the northern half of Manhattan Island, Uptown is seen as the stomping ground for the upper crust of New York. It features some of the city's most regal residences and high-end dining institutions, such as La Côte Basque. In the Upper East Side, the streets that run along Central Park – Fifth, Madison and Park Avenues – are lined with luxury boutiques and boast many of New York's cultural institutions. Across Central Park, the Upper West Side is a hive of activity of a different nature and home to many of the city's theatre and music venues.

Elizabeth Arden Red Door Spa

200 PARK AVENUE SOUTH,
UNION SQUARE

N ow a global cosmetics empire, Elizabeth Arden opened the first of her
Red Door spas in 1910. True to its name, visitors to the spa are greeted
with the eponymous fire-red tone, which is splashed throughout the interior.
The significance of the colour, which also appears across the beauty and makeup products of the brand, is a reference to the brand's iconic red lipstick – an
Arden beauty staple. Spanning two sumptuous floors, the Union Square venue
is reminiscent of a NYC townhouse mansion and is the perfect destination for
pampering and decadence before a special event. Better yet, make a visit to
indulge with a facial or massage for no reason at all.

TheMetropolitan Museum of Art

1000 FIFTH AVENUE, UPPER EAST SIDE

W hen iconic fashion editor and impresario Diana Vreeland joined The Costume Institute at the Metropolitan Museum of Art in 1973, she transformed the museum's reputation into that of a leading fashion institution. Today, as well as housing a stunning collection of historical objects from the decorative arts to clothes, the museum is host to many fashion exhibitions. The Alexander McQueen exhibition 'Savage Beauty', held in 2011, saw record-breaking attendance figures and paved the way for fashion as art. The Met Gala – an annual fundraiser and New York's foremost fashion event, which is helmed by Anna Wintour – signals the opening of the annual fashion exhibition at the Metropolitan Museum's Costume Institute. The exhibition has a year-round 'Fashion in Art' tour, which looks at costume history within the context of the museum's collections.

The Met Gala, held at the Costume Institute at the Metropolitan Museum of Art each May, is New York fashion's night of nights. Its star-studded guest list draws the hottest designers, models and Hollywood actors to the museum, and almost causes a meltdown on social media during the event. Whether it's Naomi Watts looking very Marilyn Monroe for the 2008 superhero-themed ball, or Sarah Jessica Parker's fiery headdress at the 2015 'China: Through the Looking Glass' event, gala outfits turn heads. You'll need to beg, borrow or steal to get into the gala, or you can catch up on the glamour from the comfort of your armchair on social media.

THE MET GALA
INVITATION

The Museum
at FIT

SEVENTH AVENUE AT 27TH STREET,
CHELSEA

Located at the fringe of New York's Garment District, where fabric and garment manufacturers would hustle their way from warehouse to factory floor, the Museum at FIT is a must for followers of fashion. The boundary-pushing fashion exhibitions always amaze and inspire me, offering an opportunity to get up close and personal with stunning creations by John Galliano, Alexander McQueen, Thierry Mugler, Vivienne Westwood and other fashion storytellers whose designs are housed in the museum's vast archive. Meanwhile, around the corner at the prestigious Parsons School of Design, fashion's up-and-comers ply their skills for a chance to make it in the industry.

The Museum at FIT

Fashion Week

NEW YORK – VARIOUS LOCATIONS

Twice a year the fashion industry flocks to the Big Apple for New York Fashion Week to witness the creative visions of the most talented designers come to life. Regardless of whether I'm sketching the show of a New York mainstay like Diane von Furstenberg or the cutting-edge brilliance of Marc Jacobs, it's always a thrill to sketch a Fashion Week show. The city is abuzz on and off the runway during Fashion Week, so make sure you make time to take in the scene between shows.

Vogue Offices

The New York *Vogue* offices are a place feared and revered, and a job here is a dream come true for any fashion hopeful vying for their first big break in the industry. Home to the most influential figures in fashion – think Anna Wintour and Grace Coddington – the global publication's US outpost, originally at Times Square, now has a home at One World Trade Center in Lower Manhattan's Financial District. The office, mythologised by the film *The Devil Wears Prada*, is best known for its infamous clothes and accessories closet which houses a dream wall-to-wall shelf of designer shoes. Standing at the foot of the building, I like to imagine the *Vogue* team working their magic, bringing together looks from the latest designer creations.

Times Square

Times Square, with its constant hustle and bustle, is one of New York's most iconic settings. From the giant billboards that overlook all the action to the many chain stores that populate the streets, Times Square is in many ways the heart of New York, connecting Midtown to the Upper East and West Sides. Standing in Times Square has always made me feel like I'm standing in the middle of a futuristic setting. It's one of the city's most popular tourist destinations, but nothing makes me feel more like I'm in New York than watching the yellow taxis fill the square before making my way up town to a Broadway show.

Chrysler Building

—

The glittering Manhattan skyline is one of the city's best-loved sights, and features a cast of some of the most iconic buildings in the world. The Chrysler Building, standing tall at 405 Lexington Avenue, is an Art Deco masterpiece, and its striking silhouette is a constant source of inspiration and awe for me. It was designed by architect William Van Alen and building works were completed in 1930 – in the heyday of the jazz era. The glorious seventy-seven-storey skyscraper was the world's tallest building until 1931 when the Empire State Building was completed. Head up to the observation deck to take in the incredible city views.

Empire State Building

350 FIFTH AVENUE, MIDTOWN

—

The Empire State Building – the Chrysler's rival, completed just one year after – is another jewel in the Manhattan Island skyline and an architectural icon from the Art Deco era. Designed by the architectural firm Shreve, Lamb & Harmon Associate, the Empire State Building was the world's tallest building for 39 years. Enjoy breathtaking views from the observatory deck on the top storey.

Downtown
SOHO/
Chelsea/
Meatpacking
District/
Greenwich
Village/
Nolita

E xploring the streets of Soho in Downtown is one of my favourite ways to take in the city and mingle among New York's art lovers. Once a working-class area, Downtown is now a well and truly gentrified New York district and showcases an array of the city's most stylish shops, art galleries and bars – including some hidden gems. Downtown is quintessentially hip; it's where you're likely to catch Marc Jacobs on his way to his studio, Solange Knowles dining at Cipriani or Caroline Issa getting snapped by street-style photographers during New York Fashion Week.

Flower District

WEST 28TH STREET
(BETWEEN SEVENTH AVENUE
AND SIXTH AVENUE),
CHELSEA

Wandering between the blooms of the Flower District is a truly New York experience. Nestled along West 28th Street in Chelsea, the row of flower wholesalers and retailers that line the street is a go-to for New York Fashion Week decorations. It's also a favourite for designers and New York's fashionable set. Florist Raquel Corvino's

28

ONE WAY

breathtaking arrangements have appeared
at countless events, featured in Mary-Kate
and Ashley Olsen's show for The Row and
graced the tables of the hottest functions in
the city. Arrive early to hustle with the florists
or wander down at a more reasonable hour
– perhaps stopping past La Bergamote for a
croissant on your way!

High Line

MEATPACKING DISTRICT, CHELSEA

Chelsea's High Line project has become a hot spot to take in the Meatpacking District surrounds, not to mention the excellent people-watching. The 2.3-kilometre-long elevated green passage, fully completed in 2014, winds across much of the district along a disused New York Central Railroad spur. Many designers, including Diane von Furstenberg, whose glass-roofed headquarters overlooks the High Line, fought to keep it as an iconic part of the city when the property owners proposed the High Line's demolition. The stretch is lined with stunning foliage and public art, and has become a promenade for fashion folk and street-style bloggers. During summer, Le Bain, the rooftop bar of The Standard Hotel, which straddles the south end of the High Line, is *the* place to be before and after sun goes down over the skyline.

MANOLO BLAHNIK

Carrie Bradshaw Stoop

66 PERRY STREET,
WEST VILLAGE

The image of Carrie Bradshaw, high-heeled and dressed to perfection as she heads out to a glamorous event, or in search of love in New York, is one every style-inclined person will know. Whether Carrie is sitting with her girlfriends or saying goodbye to Big, those iconic stairs have played host to many amazing outfits over the years. Remember the to-die-for slinky John Galliano newspaper dress from season three, the stunning Prada cocktail frock she wore to meet Berger in season six, or the post-fight shredded Roberto Cavalli from season four? The stoop, which is set in the Upper East Side on the show, is actually located in the West Village. For the full *Sex and the City* experience, pop by Magnolia Bakery around the corner on Bleecker Street, but be prepared to wait in line for Carrie's beloved cupcakes!

Artists Space

38 GREENE STREET,
THIRD FLOOR, SOHO

To brush up on all things contemporary art, I always add Artists Space to my New York travel calendar. Founded in 1972 by Trudie Grace and Irving Sandler, the not-for-profit gallery remains a contemporary art institution and platform for the avant-garde art scene. Having shown works by some of the biggest names in the art world, from Cindy Sherman and Barbara Kruger to Jeff Koons, it continues to host a busy exhibition and events schedule that showcases alternative art practices. Artists Space is the perfect place to get lost and find a little inspiration.

Brooklyn
Bridge Walk

L ooking at the Brooklyn Bridge from Manhattan always
   ignites a flicker of romance in me, reminding me
of films like Frank Sinatra's *It Happened in Brooklyn* and
Woody Allen's New York classic *Manhattan*. Completed in
1883, the hybrid cable-stayed/suspension bridge spans the
East River and unites the once working-class but now uber-
hip borough of Brooklyn with Manhattan Island. Strolling
across the bridge – day or night – gives one of the most
stunning views of the skyline and is one of my favourite
ways to take in the city.

Movie Premiere

BROADWAY,
UPPER WEST SIDE

:PREN

RE

It's no secret New York is home to some of the biggest names in the film business, but it's when the theatres of Manhattan roll out their red carpets for opening screenings that the city's hottest celebrities come out of the woodwork and into the Upper West Side. If you're lucky enough to get your hands on a ticket to a premiere, don't arrive too early; timing your arrival perfectly means you might get to walk the red carpet with the biggest names in film.

Broadway Show

BROADWAY THEATER DISTRICT, MIDTOWN

One of the most quintessential New York experiences is to see a show on Broadway – or The Great White Way, as it's also known. Wandering through the dazzling lights of the iconic strip, I like to picture the stylish flappers and cabaret stars of the 1920s from productions by Ziegfeld Follies with stars Louise Brooks and Marilyn Miller. In 1969 there was even a Broadway show dedicated to Coco Chanel, immortalising the designer's life on stage. The show starred Katharine Hepburn in the latest Chanel collections and featured a finale showcasing Chanel designs from 1918 to 1959. These days, the strip is a glittering spectacle with productions drawing many to the iconic tourist destination.

RADIO CIT

ROCKETTES

02

Barneys New York

660 MADISON AVENUE, MIDTOWN

After pawning his wife's engagement ring to finance the venture, Barney Pressman opened his first store in Manhattan in 1923. Barneys has since grown to become the leading luxury department store it is today. Their Madison Avenue flagship has been instrumental in pioneering New York fashion as well as introducing European imports

like Giorgio Armani to New Yorkers. The store remains a favourite with the fashion set of New York. Boundary-pushing campaigns by photographers like Juergen Teller and Bruce Weber; theatrical collaborations with Lady Gaga and Daphne Guinness; and a boutique selection of high-end and emerging designers ensures Barneys remains a retail institution.

Chanel

139 SPRING STREET,
SOHO

A longside the brand's dominating flagship in Midtown, Chanel's Soho store also brings a little bit of French haute couture to New York. With a fit out by architecture guru Peter Marino, the boutique encapsulates all the covetable hallmarks of the brand and Karl Lagerfeld's inspiring vision. The House of Chanel signatures – such as the iconic Chanel tweed and the black and white palette – can all be found at the luxury house's more intimate New York store.

Bergdorf
Goodman

754 FIFTH AVENUE,
MIDTOWN

A shopping mecca for any visitor to New York, Bergdorf Goodman is home to the infamous 'Bergdorf Blondes'. Set across ten levels, the stunning Art Deco building houses a hefty rolodex of all the luxury standards, from New York favourites like Carolina Herrera, Narcisso Rodriguez, Tamara Mellon and Derek Lam to covetable imports, such as Givenchy, Lanvin, Manolo Blahnik and Kenzo. The store's status as a design career-maker was even immortalised in the documentary *Scatter My Ashes at Bergdorf's*. As well as admiring the to-die-for fashions, make a pit stop at the BG Restaurant on level seven and enjoy the view of Central Park. With a stunning Kelly Wearstler-designed interior, it's the perfect place to treat yourself. My favourite dish on the menu is the lobster salad.

Dior

Christian Dior

21 EAST 57TH STREET,
MIDTOWN

A massive Lady Dior bag covered the scaffolding on Christian Dior's New York flagship during its renovations by architect Peter Marino. Now complete, the luxury brand's Midtown mecca attracts devotees of the brand and stocks all things Dior – from beauty and accessories to high-end men's and women's looks, hot off the runway. The stunning interior blends whimsical floral graphics with ornate classical details, bringing a little bit of Paris haute couture to Manhattan Island.

Bloomingdale's

1000 THIRD AVENUE, 59TH STREET AND
LEXINGTON AVENUE, MIDTOWN

Founded in 1872, Bloomingdale's was one of New York's first department stores, and remains a much-loved shopping destination. Inside the store's Deco exterior, which spans the block, complete with a line of fluttering flags, an overwhelming selection of the latest fashions, beauty and homewares are on offer over nine levels. Their shoe department is a personal favourite for finding that perfect pair, so it's fitting that this is where Sarah Jessica Parker launched her recent shoe collection SJP. In 2004 the department store ventured downtown, opening its Soho outpost. It's no wonder Manhattan is dotted with the iconic Bloomingdale's brown bags. Ten years ago I designed an edition of the Bloomingdale's shopper bag, and it still brings a smile to my face to see it on their shelves today!

Michael
Kors

O riginally hailing from Long Island, the king of New York fashion and former *Project Runway* host, Karl Anderson, Jr., aka Michael Kors, built his business of sportswear luxe in 1981, fresh out of New York's Fashion Institute of Technology. Today, the jetsetting Kors woman (and man) can get their fix at the designer's flagship on 520 Broadway in Soho, which carries everything from the designer's ready-to-wear, to chic leathergoods and perfume. Ever at the fore of new technology, Michael Kors' watches and mobile accoutrements are also available at the store – they're the perfect accessories for the tech-savvy fashion set.

Louis Vuitton

1 EAST 57TH STREET, MIDTOWN

S ince 2004, the Louis Vuitton flagship's façade-cum-art-canvas has become an iconic destination and showcase for the brand's projects with artists and designers. In 2012, the façade was transformed into a psychedelic spotted mural in honour of the brand's collaboration with artist Yayoi Kusama. Inside, fans of the brand will find anything and everything to fulfill their Vuitton desires across five floors, from the traditional monogrammed luggage, a Vuitton hallmark, to their high-end runway fashion, and the latest 'it bag'.

UITTON

Saks Fifth Avenue

611 FIFTH AVENUE,
MIDTOWN

S aks Fifth Avenue has been kitting out Midtown's well-heeled – from bankers to businesswomen – since 1898. Marilyn Monroe famously graced its floors on a regular basis, and it's where Elvis Presley shopped for his black leather jacket, completing his look to take the rock 'n' roll world by storm. Saks Fifth Avenue now has over fifty outlets across America (and Canada), but its flagship department store remains a shopping institution for New Yorkers. Dripping with glass bubbles and designer shoes, the 10022-SHOE department on the eighth floor is a mecca for heel addicts – it even has its own zip code.

VERA WANG

Vera Wang

158 MERCER STREET, SOHO

Going from figure skating to *Vogue*, designer Vera opened her bridal salon in 1990, selling her stunning wedding gowns, which remain a hallmark of her business. Wang has since made a name for herself in all things wedding, from the dress to the registry. Classical-style pillars and floating mannequins greet shoppers and brides-to-be in the lofty but contemporary boutique on Mercer Street. The designer's elegant furnishings, tableware, evening- and ready-to-wear, as well as her exceedingly elegant bridal all find a home at her Soho boutique.

Oscar de la Renta

772 MADISON AVENUE,
UPPER EAST SIDE

In a changing world of fashion, Oscar de la Renta's elegant brand of American haute couture has remained a constant. The pale pink stone adorning the walls of the Upper East Side boutique is a nod to the designer's Dominican Republic heritage and an elegant backdrop for his beautiful frocks. Red-carpet-worthy gowns, expertly cut cocktail dresses and classy ready-to-wear are all de la Renta hallmarks that have made the designer a favourite among First Ladies from Jacqueline Kennedy to Michelle Obama, as well as with fashion insiders like Sarah Jessica Parker and Anna Wintour. Since the designer's death, Briton Peter Copping has been tasked with taking the brand into a new era.

Jimmy Choo

**699 MADISON AVENUE,
UPPER EAST SIDE**

Jimmy Choo is *the* name in shoes.
With followers from Caroline Issa, Kate
Winslet and, of course, Carrie Bradshaw, the
brand is beloved by the fashion and celebrity
set. Founding his eponymous label in 1996
with fashion entrepreneur Tamara Mellon,
the Choo trademark is the stiletto, but today
the brand – now helmed by Sandra Choi –
sells shoes and accessories for all occasions,
even sneakers. Jimmy Choo's Upper East Side
store is a destination, readying devotees to hit
the red carpet, wedding aisle or Manhattan
sidewalk.

JIMMY CHOO

ONE WAY

85

Carolina Herrera

**954 MADISON AVENUE,
UPPER EAST SIDE**

As one of New York's most celebrated designers, Carolina Herrera is all about timeless American style and is known for dressing many of the First Ladies. Urged by the 'Empress of Fashion' Diana Vreeland, the Venezuelan–American Herrera opened her business in 1980 and has since established herself as the grande dame of New York fashion. Her flagship Upper East Side boutique on Madison Avenue places her classic approach to ready-to-wear alongside her luxurious bridal designs.

87

Henri Bendel

**712 FIFTH AVENUE,
MIDTOWN**

The brown striped Henri Bendel shopping bags sported by the Uptown set are a mainstay in the luxury shopping world. The stunning Lalique windows that adorn the building's façade have made it one of the most iconic Fifth Avenue addresses. The pioneering Bendel – who set up the store in Greenwich Village in 1895 and moved it to the Uptown locale in 1913 – is credited as being the first to bring Coco Chanel to the United States. Not only have I illustrated for Henri Bendel for many years, it's also my favourite spot in New York to discover what's new in accessories.

Frédéric Fekkai

FOURTH FLOOR,
712 FIFTH AVENUE,
MIDTOWN

O ccupying the fourth floor of department store Henri Bendel, Frédéric Fekkai's exclusive flagship salon has become synonymous with the chic women of the Upper East Side who customarily have their hair coloured there. Fekkai devotees and shoppers alike come to get the Bergdorf Blonde look, or treat themselves to the salon's exclusive menu of pampering options.

Tiffany
and Co.

727 FIFTH AVENUE,
UPPER EAST SIDE

What could possibly be more New York than the image of Audrey Hepburn gazing into the windows of Tiffany & Co. in the 1961 film adaptation of Truman Capote's *Breakfast at Tiffany's*? Croissant in hand and dressed in the iconic Givenchy 'Little Black Dress' with strings of pearls slung around her neck, Hepburn is quintessentially chic. Inside Tiffany's grand Fifth Avenue address you will find the height of luxury in stunning Art Deco surrounds. Be careful though – you might just end up leaving with one of their signature Tiffany-blue boxes!

Tom Ford

845 MADISON AVENUE,
UPPER EAST SIDE

Since leaving Gucci in 2004 and setting up his eponymous label, Tom Ford has been dressing and accessorising New York's most stylish. His Uptown flagship store on Madison Avenue exemplifies the designer's sleek brand of luxury and houses everything the modern man might desire – from silk pyjamas to bespoke cufflinks. Browse the various rooms dedicated to different sartorial elements, from the 'shirt room' to the mirror-lined octagonal 'fragrance chamber'. The store also boasts a high-end bespoke suit service, which might burn a hole in your wallet: suits begin at a mere $US 5,000!

Fivestory

**18 EAST 69TH STREET,
UPPER EAST SIDE**

The overwhelmingly chic interior of boutique department store Fivestory makes even just a visit to window-shop worthwhile. Gold-trimmed panelled walls, statuesque marble and plush velvet-soft furnishings welcome shoppers into a space that feels more like an art gallery than a department store. The stunning concept store is a favourite of the fashion set and the brainchild of owner Claire Distenfeld, who opened Fivestory in 2012 and stocks a curated selection of designer wares, including Narciso Rodriguez, Proenza Schouler and Jason Wu, among a host of others. Browse at will, or make the most of the store's boutique personal shopping service for a more intimate experience.

DKNY

**420 WEST BROADWAY,
SOHO**

Donna Karan's 'Seven Easy Pieces' –
a collection she developed in 1985 for
the working, travelling New York woman –
have become part of the DNA of American
fashion. Now a global brand, DKNY's modern
and functional approach to dressing still
prevails. The New York store attracts older
Donna Karan fans as well as a younger more
urbane market.

Manolo Blahnik

**31 WEST 54TH STREET,
MIDTOWN**

The shoes of choice of *Sex and the City's* Carrie Bradshaw, 'Manolos' complete any New York uniform. Manolo Blahnik, the Spanish-born, England-based designer, has become one of the most iconic names in high-end footwear. Devotees of the designer and his eponymous brand make the trip to Midtown to get their fix – whether it's a bedazzled peep-toe, a velvet slingback or a Swarovski-studded stiletto. The unassuming façade of the store, which sits on West 54th Street, opens up to one of New York's most beautiful shoe boutiques – shoes that look like wearable works of art are displayed on pedestals.

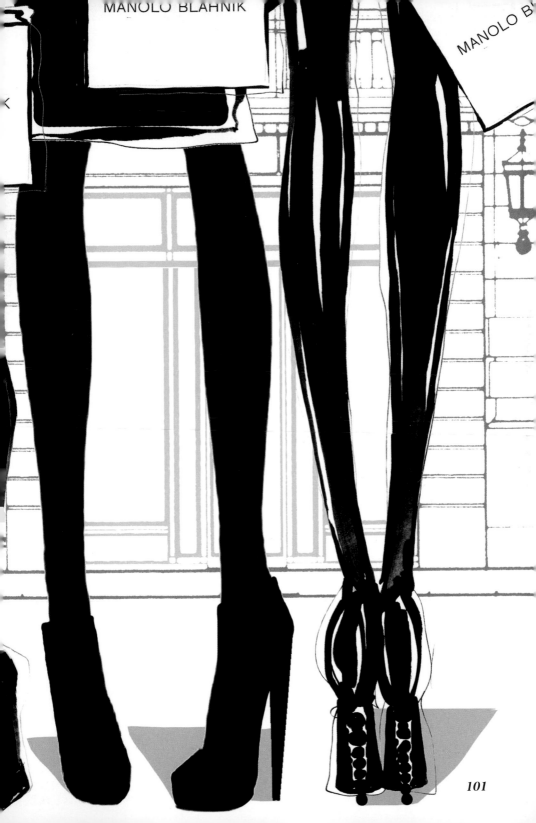

MANOLO BLAHNIK

MANOLO B'

Ralph Lauren

WOMENSWEAR:
888 MADISON AVENUE;
MENSWEAR:
867 MADISON AVENUE,
UPPER EAST SIDE

From the sporting ground to the country home, Ralph Lauren has been a pioneer of classic American style since opening up shop in 1967. The New York flagship of the now-global brand resides on Madison Avenue. The women's branch takes up number 888, and its grand four floors hold an emporium of quintessential Lauren grandeur from wall to rack. Stately displays of elegant gold-trimmed crockery, plush sofas and paintings of hunting scenes surround the clothes in the store, all of which bear the iconic Polo logo.

Jeffrey
New York

**449 WEST 14TH STREET,
MEATPACKING DISTRICT**

New York's fashion savvy flock to Jeffrey, a boutique department store that stocks a curated selection of high fashion – from European imports like Dries Van Noten, Céline and Manolo Blahnik, to local favourites such as Proenza Schouler, Kenzo and Alexander Wang. Nestled in the art gallery pocket of Chelsea's Meatpacking District, the store has prevailed despite the changing face of New York's retail landscape. Alongside Jeffrey's runway-fresh garments, its shoe department is also worthy of a visit.

Bond No. 9

399 BLEECKER STREET,
SOHO

Whether you prefer an emerald Swarovski coating or an Andy Warhol print, the graphic bottles that house the Bond No. 9 signature perfumes are sure to catch your eye. Their seasonal releases and special editions pay homage to the city of New York with names such as 'Bleecker Street Swarovski' and 'Bond No. 9 Hudson Yards'. In their exquisite store on Bleecker Street, the perfume company's unique brand of fashion-inflected pop underscores every detail – the pink-flocked chandelier floating overhead tops it off.

Aedes de Venustas

7 GREENWICH AVENUE,
WEST VILLAGE

AEDES DE VENUSTAS

New York
est. 1995

Entering the Aedes de Venustas store, visitors arrive in a Belle Époque beauty bazaar. The cult perfumery store carries a selection of curated high-end beauty brands alongside the elegant in-house range of perfumes, scented candles and body care products. The brand is part of a wave of boutique fragrance companies that are taking the city by storm. Each of Aedes's covetable bottles comes complete with the signature Venustas gold seal.

Assouline

THE PLAZA HOTEL, MEZZANINE
LEVEL, 768 FIFTH AVENUE,
MIDTOWN

Since founding their business in 1994, publishers Martine and Prosper Assouline have made their name in the business of high-end art books. Their New York store finds a home on the Plaza Hotel's mezzanine floor, overlooking the classical interior of the lobby. Complete with crystal chandeliers and a marble floor, The Plaza is a fitting setting for the luxury publisher. Lose yourself in Cecil Beaton's stunning fashion photographs, browse pages of Christian Dior's incredible creations, or catch up on cutting-edge projects in architecture and design. Abounding with titles from Assouline's elegant catalogue of art, style and photography – books that are works of art in themselves – the store also stocks a range of special editions, stationery and gift sets.

Rizzoli

**1133 BROADWAY,
NOMAD**

For the art and fashion lover, it's hard to go past Rizzoli, makers of some of the most luxurious print books ever created. Set on Broadway, in the neighbourhood of NoMad, their new flagship store houses the most beautiful coffee table tomes on art, fashion and interiors. Located on the ground floor of the 1896 Beaux Arts St. James building, the store's

high ceilings and whimsical Fornasetti wallpaper bring a sense of fairytale grandeur. Grand wooden bookshelves house the publisher's elegant collection of illustrated books as well as offering the latest in magazines. This is a store that truly pays homage to the printed page.

Marc Jacobs

**403 BLEECKER STREET,
WEST VILLAGE**

Marc Jacobs, the king of New York fashion, offers up 403 Bleecker Street as a destination for his fans to fawn over his latest offerings. At times irreverent and rebellious but always chic, Jacobs has managed to stay on the front foot in fashion over his decades-long career. His West Village store is no exception, stocking all things Jacobs from the latest collection to his tongue-in-cheek phone covers. The designer's Bleecker Street take over doesn't end at the store; be sure to make a trip to the menswear boutique and the stunning bookstore, Bookmarc, both down the street. As further testament to his domination of the locale, for his Resort 2016 collection, Jacobs even took over the streets of Soho by sending his models down a catwalk on nearby Mercer Street.

Diane von Furstenberg

874 WASHINGTON ST,
MEATPACKING DISTRICT

Diane von Furstenberg continues to reign as the powerhouse of New York fashion. Ever since the success of her famous wrap dress, a design she created in 1972 after her divorce from Prince Egon von Furstenberg, she's been dressing the power women of New York and abroad. Colourful fabrics and signature prints have become Furstenberg mainstays. Her recently built flagship studio and boutique overlooking the High Line in Manhattan's Meatpacking District has become yet another jewel in her crown. Nicknamed the 'Diamond in the Sky', the stunning building was designed in 2007 by architectural studio WORKac and features a faceted glass rooftop dome, exquisitely decorated with Swarovski crystals. The store at the bottom of the building is pure Furstenberg: New York glamour with a dash of playfulness.

Anna Sui

**484 BROOME STREET,
SOHO**

$\mathbb{N}$ ever one to shy away from colour and embellishment, Anna Sui's whimsical, decorated style transports shoppers from the street into a thrift-store inspired high-end emporium. Ever since she set up her label in the early 1980s, the Detroit-born New York-based designer's mood boards reflect a wealth of sources – from vintage fashion, bohemia and rock 'n' roll, to Victoriana and the ornate decorative arts

ANNA SUI

of her Chinese heritage. These career-long inspirations find their way into her new flagship store in Soho. The walls, painted in Sui's signature lilac, are covered in music posters and graphics from the 1960s and 1970s alongside one-of-a-kind decorative objects, which reflect the designer's irresistibly playful approach.

MoMA Design Store

81 SPRING STREET, SOHO

Popular among locals and tourists alike, the MoMA Design Store is the ultimate place to find the perfect quirky gift. It sells a curated range of designer furniture and objects including classic homewares, creative collaborations and prints from the gallery's collection – exactly what you'd expect from this leading art and design institution. Stocking iconic design heavyweights like Alvar Aalto, Mario Bellini and Charles and Ray Eames as well as newcomers like HAY, Maurizio Cattelan and Page Goolrick, the store is an emporium of art and design set across two floors. Located in an area that has become synonymous with art and design, it's my favourite spot to pick up souvenirs for friends.

Bookmarc

400 BLEECKER STREET,
WEST VILLAGE

Never one to stand still, Marc Jacobs' forays beyond fashion have seen the designer orchestrate some very exciting collaborations and projects with artists, designers and filmmakers. It's fitting then that he has ventured into the world of books in his elegant West Village art book boutique, Bookmarc. From special editions and elegant photobooks

MARC JACOBS

DON'T WALK

MARC JACOBS

BOOKMARC

to irresistible fashion monographs, the store has one of the most amazing collections of fashion books in New York. Even revered fashion editor Grace Coddington, on the re-release of her book *Thirty Years of Fashion at Vogue*, graced the Bookmarc premises for a signing; the store regularly features a host of authors and events.

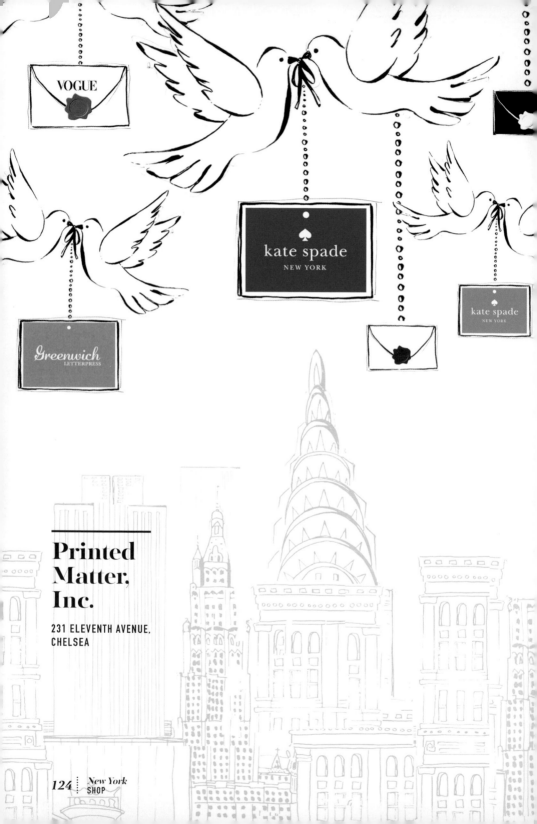

Printed
Matter,
Inc.

231 ELEVENTH AVENUE,
CHELSEA

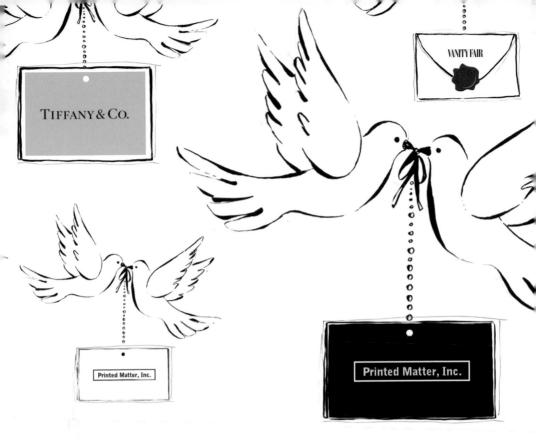

TIFFANY & CO.

VANITY FAIR

Printed Matter, Inc.

Printed Matter, Inc.

Ever since opening shop in 1976, Printed Matter, Inc. has been a beacon for independent publishing. Founded by a collective of the city's avant-garde, including Carl Andre, Sol LeWitt and Lucy Lippard, the New York institution continues to stock all things print, from art books and underground artist zines to the latest independent magazines. With over 15,000 titles stocked on its shelves, the store is the ultimate source of inspiration, whether you're browsing the cabinets of rare and out-of-print books by artists such as Jenny Holzer, Yoko Ono and Cindy Sherman, or visiting their curated exhibition space, which showcases emerging artists working in the printed space.

French Sole
fs/ny

**985 LEXINGTON AVENUE,
UPPER EAST SIDE**

When New Yorkers need to switch from heels to ballet flats, French Sole is the destination of choice and a favourite among fashion clientele like Olivia Palermo and Cindy Crawford. The brand has every imaginable variation of the ballet flat, from peep-toes to their classic 'Ingrid' flat – they even have a cork range. All shoes are made in the company's

French factory. Their store on Lexington Avenue is a go-to for sidewalk-weary feet; the walls are stocked from the ground up with ballet flats. If you can't find the perfect pair, their outlet store is across the street, and it might just have the shoes you're looking for.

127

Proenza Schouler

**822 MADISON AVENUE,
UPPER EAST SIDE**

In 2002, department store Barney's bought Jack McCollough's and Lazaro Hernandez's entire Parsons graduate collection. Ever since, the fashion designers, and their label Proenza Schouler, have become New York fashion darlings. Their unusual detailing, conceptual cutting and psychedelic prints ensure the brand remains at the forefront of the industry. Their Uptown store is every bit as chic as the designers themselves, bringing their art-meets-fashion aesthetic to life. Shoppers enter the store, which was designed by architect David Adjaye, through a wood-slatted tunnel lined with shoes and bags, which then opens up into a stark space that blends the old with the new.

Opening Ceremony

WOMENSWEAR:
35 HOWARD STREET;
MENSWEAR:
33 HOWARD STREET,
SOHO

Cool kids on the block Humberto Leon and Carol Lim took New York – and then the world – by storm when they opened their chic concept store Opening Ceremony in 2002. Their cutting-edge collaborations, business smarts and celebrity clientele make Leon and Lim a formidable team. Alongside their Los Angeles and Tokyo stores, they have twin menswear and womenswear flagships in Soho, where they stock the hottest designers from around the world, including Kenzo, Alexander Wang, Rodarte, Patrik Ervell and Proenza Schouler.

Alexander Wang

103 GRAND STREET, SOHO

Alexander Wang's luxe store on Grand Street extends the designer's edgy model-off-duty style into high fashion cool. Decked out in white marble and black leather, the space features a black mink hammock as its centrepiece. The designer's hallmarks – racy leather jackets, subdued prints, perfectly cut basics and to-die-for boots – are all within arm's reach. But the most striking feature of the store is the steel cage exhibition space at the entrance, which greets cult followers with a rotating display presenting the concept of the latest collection. The approach makes Wang a fitting addition to the unique art and high fashion crowd of Downtown.

ALEXANDER WANG

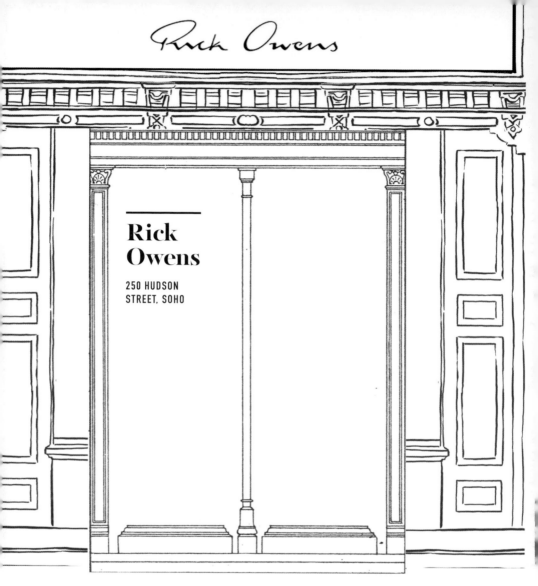

Rick
Owens

250 HUDSON STREET, SOHO

Originally from California, and now Paris-based, Rick Owens and his sartorial partner in crime, Michelle Lamy, have regularly pushed the boundaries with their provocative and avant-garde designs that question fashion. But there's also an underlying elegance to the Owens brand that translates seamlessly into their stunning store in Soho. The sombre colour palette, high white walls and displays that honour elemental materials – from the concrete floor to the blocks of sandstone seating – all highlight this sophistication. Dramatic basics, quintessential drapery and cocoon-like leather jackets – all Rick Owens hallmarks – fill the racks of this starkly modern Downtown space.

135

rag &
bone

**104 CHRISTOPHER STREET,
WEST VILLAGE**

Marcus Wainwright and David Neville started rag & bone with a simple pair of jeans. Their edgy tailoring, chic basics and effortlessly cool leather outerwear have become bookends of the rag & bone ranges. The label now epitomises the new face of Downtown. Always at the front foot of fashion, rag & bone regularly collaborates with the hottest names in fashion and art, from fashion photographer Glen Luchford to Swedish street artist Rubin, and a host of others. The West Village store, opened in 2008, stocks their men's and women's ranges in an industrial setting of exposed brick walls, fittings fabricated from steel piping and factory-style light shades.

Jonathan
Adler

53 GREENE STREET,
SOHO

Potter turned interior design guru Jonathan Adler has gone from strength to strength since launching his first ceramic collection in 1993 at Barneys. His Soho flagship on Greene Street, which he opened in 1998, has a stunning selection of lighting, furniture and homewares that reflect the designer's unique sensibility: colourful, modern and always irreverent. When he's not at the wheel churning out his tongue-in-cheek cookie jars or quirky animal figures, Adler is enjoying his celebrity status on the design scene, or writing. His books – such as *My Prescription for Anti-Depressive Living* – bring the designer's cheeky humour to the printed page.

SOHO

ONE WAY

ONE

DONT
WALK

Chelsea Flea Market

BETWEEN SIXTH AVENUE AND
BROADWAY WEST 25TH STREET,
CHELSEA

T he Chelsea Flea Market, a favourite of locals and tourists alike, is the perfect pit stop after walking the High Line. It's abundant with antiques, clothing, jewellery and retro bric-a-brac; you'll get lost foraging for that vintage one-of-a-kind piece to take home. With the market held every Saturday and Sunday, there is no excuse not to spend the New York weekend browsing vintage Murano glasswear, mid-century costume jewellery, exotic Middle Eastern rugs, stunning Irish linen and other treasures on offer at the open-air market.

From ~ $200

Brooklyn Flea

SATURDAY: FORT GREENE FLEA
AT 176 LAFAYETTE AVENUE,
FORT GREENE

SUNDAY: DUMBO FLEA AT
MANHATTAN BRIDGE ARCHWAY
PLAZA, BROOKLYN

SUNDAY: GRAND ARMY MARKET
AT GRAND ARMY PLAZA,
PROSPECT PARK

W hether it's finding that rare piece for the home, shopping for last-minute gifts or browsing for the perfect vintage dress, I love venturing across the Brooklyn Bridge for some good old-fashioned bargain hunting. Operating several markets over the weekend, Brooklyn Flea hosts a curated selection of vendors in different locations throughout the borough. Spend your Saturday wandering through the aisles at Fort Greene Flea, or Sunday at DUMBO Flea under Manhattan Bridge Archway Plaza or at the newly established Grand Army Market at the northern tip of Prospect Park. As well as browsing the eclectic clothes, chic furniture and bric-a-brac on offer, you'll also enjoy the people-watching – the markets are a veritable hub for hip local street style. If that's not enough to draw you there, the edible delights on offer at the food stalls will make the weekend journey worthwhile.

Sleep

The Carlyle &
The Empire Hotel

**35 EAST 76TH STREET, UPPER EAST SIDE /
44 WEST 63RD STREET, UPPER WEST SIDE**

One of New York's Art Deco landmarks, named in honour of British literary figure Thomas Carlyle, The Carlyle hotel is a haven of understated elegance. The sumptuous chandeliers and brightly coloured velvet sofas create a stunning setting, conceived by anti-minimalist interior stylist Dorothy Draper. White-gloved concierge and elevator staff in impeccable uniforms embody the discreet charm of the hotel, which has been cherished by generations of clientele, from famed political figures and royalty to fashion and film elite. Across town, The Empire Hotel is also a favourite of the rich and famous. Another Art Deco landmark, the luxury hotel's interior is as eclectic as its guests. The Empire's stunning rooftop, aglow under the 'Hotel Empire' neon sign, is an essentially New York setting.

The Surrey

**20 EAST 76TH STREET,
UPPER EAST SIDE**

A boutique luxury hotel, the Surrey combines Art Deco–style with modern aesthetics. Bar Pleiades, one of the hotel's luxurious dining venues, takes inspiration from fashion designer and modernist Coco Chanel. The timeless elegance of the interior reinforces the designer's mantra that 'simplicity is the keynote of all true elegance.' Just a block away from Central Park, the Metropolitan Museum and other cultural landmarks, the Uptown hotel also boasts an impressive collection of modern and contemporary art, including works by Jenny Holzer, Richard Serra, and Chuck Close's filmic portrait of Kate Moss that overlooks the foyer. Guests can request a tour of the collection housed by the hotel.

The Plaza Hotel

768 FIFTH AVENUE, MIDTOWN

Guests of The Plaza enter via the red carpet, rolled out across the sidewalk, to be greeted by the white-gloved concierge staff. The epic hotel, completed in 1907, was the first in the city to be designated as a landmark. It features a gilded Beaux Arts interior that conjures old New York, and suite names, such as the 'Pulitzer Suite' and the 'Ellington Suite'. F. Scott Fitzgerald set scenes of The Great Gatsby in the hotel. The Plaza has seen many of Manhattan's rich and famous grace its rooms, from presidents to Hollywood starlets. The Beatles, Eleanor Roosevelt, Mark Twain and Groucho Marx were among its many star-studded guests over the years. The iconic Grand Ballroom, completed in 1929, with a luxurious Art Deco interior of gold-accented panels and grand chandeliers, is pure Gatsby. Today, it is one of the most prestigious wedding venues in the city, and back in 1966 it was the venue for Truman Capote's infamous 'Black and White' masked ball, which was nicknamed the 'Party of the Century'.

Baccarat Hotel & Residences

28 WEST 53RD STREET, MIDTOWN

—

As one of New York's newest hotel additions, the Baccarat is fast becoming a favourite for luxury travellers. Only a stone's throw from MoMA, the hotel brings a taste of luxury and French glamour to Midtown with Baccarat crystal at every turn. After entering into the glittering building, guests are greeted with a breathtaking interior, the creation of Paris-based designers Gilles & Bossier. The stunning Harcourt Wall – an illuminated wall of two thousand Harcourt 1841 glasses; the Baccarat glassware that decks the tables of restaurant Chevalier; and the decadent chandeliers that hang throughout the building all contribute to the glamorous appeal of the hotel. The Baccarat is also the home of the first ever La Mer Spa. Expect to see Zac Posen, Bobbi Brown and others of the fashion elite at this luxury venue, which plays host to some of fashion's hottest events.

153

The Ace Hotel
Gramercy Park Hotel
The Royalton
Waldorf Astoria

20 WEST 29TH STREET, MIDTOWN /
2 LEXINGTON AVENUE, GRAMERCY /
44 WEST 44TH STREET, MIDTOWN /
301 PARK AVENUE, MIDTOWN

The only struggle you'll have in finding a bed in Midtown will be choosing which one. Dotted throughout the district are some of the city's most luxurious places to spend the night. There's the uber trendy Ace Hotel, a hotspot for young, hip freelancers and creative types. Or there's the Gramercy Park Hotel – its curated vintage-inspired interior and bespoke furniture by artist Julian Schnabel is famed for celebrity-studded parties. The equally luxe boutique hotel The Royalton, originally fitted out by Philippe Starck, attracts New York City's business and fashion elite. For a truly indulgent Manhattan night's sleep, the Waldorf Astoria must be one of the city's best-loved luxury hotels. Founded in 1893, it's been the choice for silver screen starlets like Marilyn Monroe and was a happening jazz club during the 1950s and 1960s. It boasts a celebrity guest list, amenities designed by Salvatore Ferragamo and a famous restaurant known for the New York classic, the Waldorf Salad.

WALDORF ASTORIA®
NEW YORK

155

The St. Regis Hotel New York

2 EAST 55TH STREET AT FIFTH AVENUE, MIDTOWN

For a taste of real New York luxury it's hard to go past the St. Regis New York in Midtown. The stunning surrounds of the Beaux Arts building on East 55th Street – built in 1904 by John Jacob Astor – makes walking up the red-carpeted stairs to the hotel's foyer feel like the height of glamour. Visit the King Cole Bar for a martini, or stay the night in their bespoke Dior Suite. The room, nestled on the twelfth floor, takes inspiration from the Dior atelier in Paris, and is kitted out with attention to detail reminiscent of the house's haute couture garments. Louis XVI-style furniture set against silk and velvet draping in soft greys, and walls featuring watercolour fashion illustrations, make this suite a truly luxury experience.

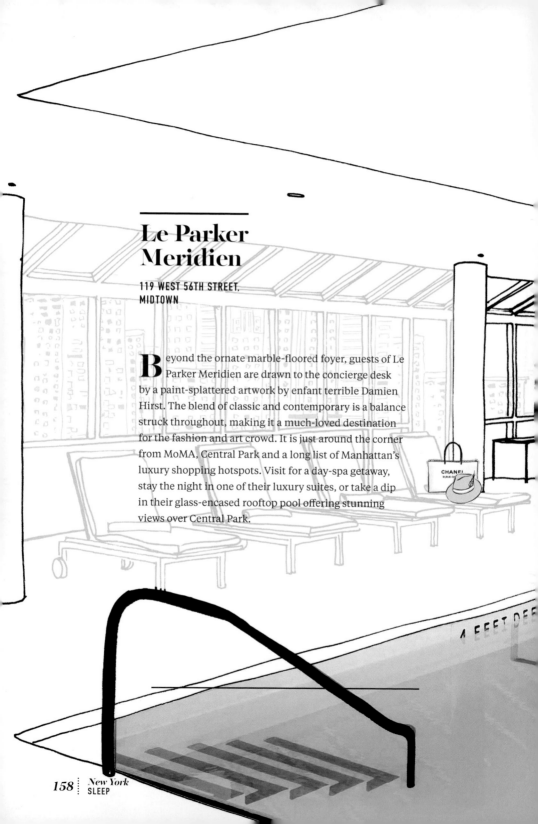

Le Parker Meridien

119 WEST 56TH STREET, MIDTOWN

Beyond the ornate marble-floored foyer, guests of Le Parker Meridien are drawn to the concierge desk by a paint-splattered artwork by enfant terrible Damien Hirst. The blend of classic and contemporary is a balance struck throughout, making it a much-loved destination for the fashion and art crowd. It is just around the corner from MoMA, Central Park and a long list of Manhattan's luxury shopping hotspots. Visit for a day-spa getaway, stay the night in one of their luxury suites, or take a dip in their glass-encased rooftop pool offering stunning views over Central Park.

Four Seasons & Hudson

57 EAST 57TH STREET, MIDTOWN /
358 WEST 58TH STREET, MIDTOWN

HUDSON
NEW YORK

The iconic Four Seasons hotel chain finds its New York home on East 57th Street in the heart of the island. Across the street from Tiffany's and a host of other stores in the luxury shopping district, the 52-storey, five-star luxury hotel stands tall over Midtown, with rooms that offer incredible views of the city. Just blocks away, the stylish Hudson hotel offers beds for the design-savvy. With a concrete and neon glass façade, and a hyper-styled interior by famed designer Philippe Starck, the hotel epitomises 'Cheap Chic' style, with details that poke fun at design tradition. A luminous glass escalator transports guests to the first-floor lobby. The hotel's many event spaces make it the perfect choice for some of the city's hottest fashion and film parties.

Soho Grand Hotel & Sixty Soho & Nomo Soho & The Standard & The Maritime Hotel & The Greenwich Hotel

310 WEST BROADWAY, SOHO / 60 THOMPSON STREET, SOHO / 9 CROSBY STREET, SOHO / 848 WASHINGTON STREET, MEATPACKING DISTRICT / 363 WEST 16TH STREET, CHELSEA / 377 GREENWICH STREET, TRIBECA

—

With the best of New York's art and fashion scene at your doorstep, Soho's luxury hotel offering leaves little to be desired. Some of my favourites are Soho Grand and Sixty Soho, both of which offer indulgence in an intimate setting. Nomo Soho is the place to be during New York Fashion Week; it's where all the bloggers, photographers, models – and anyone who's anyone – stay during the event. The Standard continues to make its mark as the new generation in luxury, attracting New York's up-and-coming creatives – the venue is where Jay-Z and Solange Knowles famously had their elevator showdown at the Met Gala after-party. Around the corner, the distinctive porthole exterior of The Maritime Hotel, an iconic mid-century architectural landmark overlooking The High Line, is a unique experience in itself. Robert De Niro's Greenwich Hotel offers a more classic option and is a favourite of the film and fashion industry.

Crosby
Street Hotel

79 CROSBY STREET, SOHO

The brainchild of London hoteliers Tim and Kit Kemp, Crosby Street Hotel is both creative and cosy. Kit's decor mixes quirky design detailing with colourful vintage elements. The boutique hotel is the New York fashion industry's venue of choice for fittings and hair and makeup for events such as the annual Met Gala, with celebrated stars and major fashion houses booking into Crosby Street. During a stay you might find yourself lounging in one of the hotel's gorgeous loft-inspired spaces, or perhaps wandering through the luscious rooftop garden, which supplies the downstairs restaurant with fresh produce.

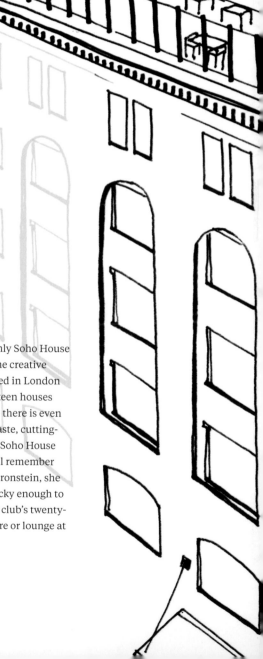

Soho House

**29-35 NINTH AVENUE,
MEATPACKING DISTRICT**

Around the world, the discreet members-only Soho House has a notoriously illustrious clientele in the creative industries. The private venue, which was founded in London in 1995 by entrepreneur Nick Jones, now has fifteen houses in major global cities from Toronto to Istanbul – there is even a country house in Oxfordshire, UK. Exquisite taste, cutting-edge interiors, discretion and exclusivity are all Soho House trademarks. If you're a *Sex and the City* fan you'll remember that even when Samantha posed as Annabelle Bronstein, she still couldn't secure a membership. If you are lucky enough to make it into the luxury venue, stay in one of the club's twenty-four guest rooms, visit the intimate movie theatre or lounge at the rooftop pool.

04

Little Collins

667 LEXINGTON AVE. MIDTOWN

Little Collins is one of my favourite places to get coffee in New York. Australian owner-enrepreneur Leon Unglik, who opened the café in 2013, also offers Vegemite toast alongside lattes. Even if Vegemite isn't to your taste, the menu of brunch staples like bircher muesli, smashed avocado and coffee done well make this over-the-counter café a favourite of New Yorkers and Aussie expats alike. Drop in to charge up before you spend the day exploring New York.

171

MarieBelle
New York
Chocolates

484 BROOME ST, SOHO

The petit ganache-centred squares, decorated with a stunning vintage graphic, that are sold at MarieBelle are works of art. Tucked away on Broome Street, the Soho boutique of this quaint chocolatier is the perfect place to enjoy a rich hot chocolate or some decadent treats. Opened by Maribel Lieberman in 2002, the store is as much a feast for the eyes as it is for the taste buds. A background in fashion gave Lieberman a taste for interiors; the store is a wonderland of mixed vintage elements, from an Art Nouveau cabinet to the MarieBelle signature blue diamond-pattern wallpaper.

173

Magnolia Bakery

401 BLEECKER STREET, SOHO

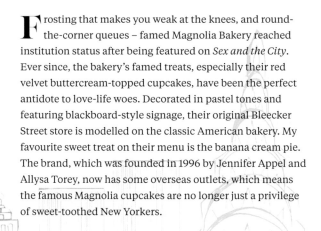

Frosting that makes you weak at the knees, and round-the-corner queues – famed Magnolia Bakery reached institution status after being featured on *Sex and the City*. Ever since, the bakery's famed treats, especially their red velvet buttercream-topped cupcakes, have been the perfect antidote to love-life woes. Decorated in pastel tones and featuring blackboard-style signage, their original Bleecker Street store is modelled on the classic American bakery. My favourite sweet treat on their menu is the banana cream pie. The brand, which was founded in 1996 by Jennifer Appel and Allysa Torey, now has some overseas outlets, which means the famous Magnolia cupcakes are no longer just a privilege of sweet-toothed New Yorkers.

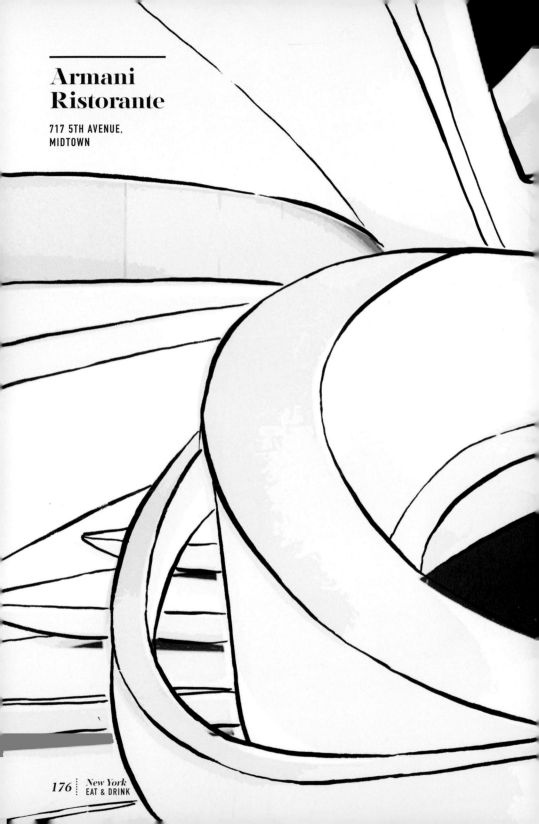

Armani
Ristorante

717 5TH AVENUE,
MIDTOWN

Fashion meets food at this elegant incarnation of the Armani brand. A sculptural staircase, designed by architects Doriana and Massimiliano Fuksas, connects the entrance foyer of the Armani store to the upstairs dining area. The modern luxury of the Milanese brand is evident in every element of the restaurant, from the exquisite fare offered to the monochrome colour palette. Guests are even served Armani's very own sparkling water – Acqua Armani.

ARMANI / RISTORANTE

ARMANI

BG Restaurant at Bergdorf Goodman

LEVEL 7, 754 FIFTH AVENUE, MIDTOWN

One of my all-time favourite commissions involved drawing the BG restaurant for Bergdorf Goodman. After a day of pounding the sidewalk, the BG Restaurant on level seven of the department store is the perfect refuge. The stunning interior, designed by Kelly Wearstler, is pure *Alice In Wonderland*, with curved leather chairs, a chequerboard floor and a pastel colour palette – all overlooking Central Park. The Gotham Salad on the lunch menu is a specialty, and a favourite of the fashion cognoscenti who frequent the venue.

Grand Central Oyster Bar & Restaurant

**GRAND CENTRAL TERMINAL,
89 EAST 42ND ST, MIDTOWN**

The evocative Grand Central Oyster, with its vaulted, intricately tiled ceiling and red-chequered tablecloths, continues to bustle with locals and in-the-know tourists alike. In the cellar of Manhattan's Grand Central Terminal, oysters arrive on ice by the dozen in abundant platters and the champagne flows. For a more low-key meal, try a lunch of bloody marys and lobster rolls. The meeting of old and new in this iconic venue makes it a popular setting for Fashion Week parties and designer photo shoots. For his spring/summer 2015 collection, designer Jason Wu shot a campaign featuring model Karlie Kloss lounging on the venue's main bar alongside a Grand Central lobster roll.

The
Beatrice Inn

285 WEST 12TH STREET, WEST VILLAGE

—

Since its heady days as a popular speakeasy club in the 1920s, The Beatrice Inn has attracted Manhattan's hottest crowd. During its more recent club days, it was frequented by fashion insiders, designers, stylists and editors, who regularly brought the venue to the pages of fashion magazines by hosting some of New York Fashion Week's best parties there; guest lists include Mary-Kate and Ashley Olsen, Kate Moss and Chloë Sevigny among others. It was recently reignited by restaurant guru and *Vanity Fair* editor Graydon Carter, who transformed the venue into a high-end meat-heavy brasserie that continues to attract a star-studded list of clientele.

Balthazar

80 SPRING STREET,
SOHO

Balthazar is a bustling institution for Manhattan's Francophiles and a spot at which it's notoriously hard to secure a table. The brasserie offers a menu of French standards, from pommes frites to steak tartare, in a warm interior of wood-panelled walls, sparkling mirrors and red leather booths that will transport you to another time and place. The venue provides relief for Parisian expats, as well as being a destination for fashion and celebrity clientele like Victoria and David Beckham, Julianne Moore and Sophia Loren. Without a doubt, this is my favourite New York restaurant.

La Bergamote

177 NINTH AVENUE,
CHELSEA

While famed for their croissants, croque monsieurs and quiches, it's La Bergamote's sweet treats that really steal the show. The glass cabinet of irresistible French pastries on offer at this Chelsea bakery is a sight to behold, from the individually moulded towers of strawberry mousse to the decadent chocolate éclairs. The only problem is which one to choose!

Bar Pitti
& Cipriani
Downtown
& Il Cantinori

268 SIXTH AVENUE, WEST VILLAGE /
376 WEST BROADWAY, SOHO /
32 EAST 10TH STREET, GREENWICH
VILLAGE

It's no secret New Yorkers love their Italian, from the New York slice to the boutique trattorias frequented by the city's fashionable set. One of my favourite haunts, Bar Pitti, has been serving up traditional Tuscan fare since 1992, and attracts a celebrity clientele to its sidewalk tables to feast on seasonal specials. I also love Cipriani Downtown, an elegant and popular lunch spot for New York's movers and shakers. A collection of famed artworks adorns the walls, while white tablecloths create a refined dining atmosphere. Cipriani's Bellini, a house specialty, is the perfect aperitif. Il Cantinori is another must on the list of Italian dining destinations. From the terracotta-tiled floor and stunning floral arrangements to the Risotto Pescatori, Il Cantinori fulfils the brief of a classic Tuscan trattoria. Its fresh seasonal menu has meant the restaurant has kept diners returning since opening in 1983. So much so that the venue was famously featured as the choice for Carrie's forlorn thirty-fifth birthday in *Sex and the City*. I have to say that my nights there have always had a happier ending!

Bottino

246 TENTH AVENUE, CHELSEA

—

In the heart of the gallery district and a stone's throw from the High Line, Bottino regularly attracts influential players in New York's art and fashion scene. The high-end restaurant, which was opened in 1998 by Danny Emerman and Alessandro Prosperi, serves up contemporary Tuscan cuisine to its loyal followers. Like many Downtown venues, it has a stunning garden area that becomes a magical, ivy-surrounded, candlelit wonderland after sunset. The interior of the restaurant is more pared back; mid-century wooden furniture and restrained decoration make this the perfect locale for a working lunch or dinner if you're looking to brush shoulders with gallerists, artists and curators of the local art scene.

The
Waverly Inn
and Garden

16 BANK STREET,
WEST VILLAGE

N ow in the hands of *Vanity Fair* editor and restaurant
impresario Graydon Carter, The Waverly Inn has been
a New York mainstay since opening its doors in 1920. These
days, getting a table isn't easy, but if you're lucky enough
to secure a sought-after spot, you'll find a menu of simple,
modern French-influenced fare. Dinner at The Waverly offers
a candlelit atmosphere with white tablecloths and impeccable
cocktails. The stunning garden room at the back of the venue
is the perfect setting for a glamorous New York lunch.

193

The King Cole Bar at the St. Regis

2 EAST 55TH STREET,
AT FIFTH AVENUE, MIDTOWN

Martinis are a must in Midtown and The King Cole Bar knows how they're done. Located on the ground floor of the gorgeous St. Regis Hotel, the bar evokes the swinging New York jazz era of the 1920s with an Art Deco interior and a giant mural behind the bar. A pre-dinner visit to The King Cole Bar is the perfect way to relax after a busy day spent exploring Midtown's stunning luxury shopping district.

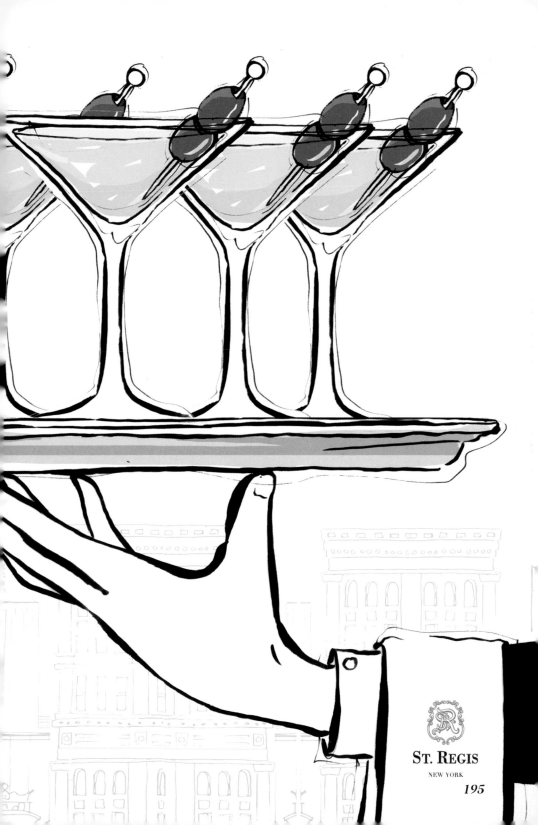

ST. REGIS

NEW YORK

195

Salon De Ning at the Peninsula Hotel

LEVEL 23, 700 FIFTH AVENUE, MIDTOWN

With breathtaking views, the Salon De Ning rooftop bar at the Peninsula Hotel is the perfect way to take in the Manhattan skyline at night. Named after Madame Ning, a fictional Shanghai socialite of the 1930s, the oriental bar will transport you to another era. With elegant Cheongsam dresses enclosed in glass cabinets and spectacular artwork, the interior playfully evokes the jazz era. But if you get carried away, catching a glimpse of the soaring Manhattan skyscrapers will bring you right back to New York.

The Back Room & Schiller's Liquor Bar

131 RIVINGTON STREET,
LOWER EAST SIDE /
102 NORFOLK STREET,
LOWER EAST SIDE

A cocktail den, The Back Room keeps up the spirit of its history as a prohibition-era venue by making visitors enter through the same secret entrance that was used during the 1920s. Plush red velvet and jacquard soft furnishings, wood-panelled walls, red lampshades and dim lighting give the venue an intimate speakeasy atmosphere. So much so that it was featured on HBO's hit television drama *Boardwalk Empire*. Another haunt for cocktail connoisseurs is the nearby Schiller's Liquor Bar established in 2003. In addition to their famed drinks, owner Keith McNally and chef Shane McBride have been serving up home-style bistro cooking to their loyal diners, making the bar a favourite for the gastronomically inclined.

The Chef's Table at Brooklyn Fare

200 SCHERMERHORN STREET, BROOKLYN

There may be a six-week waitlist for The Chef's Table at Brooklyn Fare, but the covetable dining venue is worth the wait. The three-Michelin-starred, fine dining restaurant, opened by César Ramírez in 2009, is one of the city's favourites. The spaced is decorated with hanging luminous copper pots, and seafood is the focus of a rotating tasting menu that draws from French and Japanese influences. Diners enjoy food straight from the chef's U-shaped steel counter that extends through the restaurant.